"Physician, soldier, mother and one who sees the world, not because it is beautiful but because it needs us. Dr Ritchie has brought us to her world, a world more need to see and understand."
Robert J. Ursano, M.D.
Professor of Psychiatry and Neuroscience,
Chair, Dept of Psychiatry,
Uniformed Services University of the Health Sciences

"Military medicine has evolved dramatically over the decades since the Vietnam War. Colonel Cam Ritchie's poetry and commentaries focus on the support of more recent operations from the perspective of soldiers deployed worldwide. She brings a human face to Army medicine."
George K. Anderson, MD,
MPH, Major General, USAF, MC (retired),
Executive Director, AMSUS

"A truly outstanding compilation of poems which poignantly conveys the raw emotion elicited when confronting life's challenges. Colonel Ritchie utilizes a wealth of personal experience as a Soldier, Physician, teacher, therapist, spouse, and parent during a distinguished twenty-eight year career as an Army Psychiatrist to illustrate her feelings vividly."
C.J. Diebold, MD

"A poignant and impassioned collection of poems and prose pieces that span a distinguished career as an Army psychiatrist, they evoke the challenges and fulfillment in caring for patients during war-- war defined not solely on the battlefield, but on the HIV wards and ICU's. Dr. Ritchie opens our eyes to her world full of emotion and shares her heart that is honest and evocative."
COL Ron Poropatich, MD – US Army Medical Department

"It is a privilege when one allows another to care for them – this privilege extended into a professional career for Army psychiatrist Col. Elspeth Cameron Ritchie. The people whom she touched through her medical work ignited her creativity to examine another side of life and intimacy through prose and poetry. This artistic collection will enhance the shelf of medical professionals, students and others who seek to understand the human condition. A job well done."
Dori Reissman. MD, MPH (CAPT, USPHS).Senior Medical Advisor,
Office of the Director, NIOSH

"This book is a powerful mixture of experience, expertise and sensitivity of a woman psychiatrist who understands the serious psychological challenges facing an all-volunteer armed forces."
   John A. Parrish, M.D.

"Written through the lens of a military physician, this book of poems captures beautifully the world of a sensitive doctor, a war-weary combat soldier, a devoted daughter, loving mother and wife; most of all it tells the world of the remarkable journey of a professional woman asked to witness the most difficult things life can offer. Resilience to the effects of traumatic events is the highlight of this impeccable collection; the stories are a triumph of one woman's spirit."
   Terry Keane, Ph.D.,
   Associate Chief of Staff for Research & Development,
   VA Boston Healthcare System, Director: Behavioral Science Division,
   National Center for Posttraumatic Stress Disorder

"The Nation knows Dr. (COL) Elspeth Cameron Ritchie as a military mental health expert, an outspoken advocate for our Soldiers and veterans, and a dedicated and confident professional medical officer. Tearing at the Moon shows another side –the thoughtful observer of suffering, loss and human spirit. Dr. Ritchie's poems and essays explore what might lie beneath the tough exterior of any hardworking physician, brave patient or hardened soldier. They reveal her very personal experience with war and its aftermath, with illness, injury, fear and death. Her prosaic soul-searching also suggests a motivation for her years of selfless service to the Army Medical Corps."
   David M. Benedek, M.D.COL,
   MC, USA, Professor/Deputy Chair & Assoc. Director/Senior Scientist,
   Center for the Study of Traumatic Stress, Dept. of Psychiatry,
   Uniformed Services University of the Health Sciences

"Soldier...physician...psychiatrist...poet...all deserve respect but in combination demands admiration. This collection reveals Colonel Ritchie's brilliant insights into the most complex and complicated human emotions surrounding duty, death, love, and compassion as lived and understood by a warrior healer. Sometimes bold, sometimes raw, sometimes enigmatic but ever compelling for glimpses of lives and stories that lie just beyond the verse and prose. Well done."
   Colonel Bruce E. Crow, Psy.D. Clinical Psychology Consultant to the
   U.S. Army Surgeon General; Director, Warrior Resiliency Program,
   Southern Regional Medical Command, Ft. Sam Houston, Texas

Tearing Through the Moon:

Poems & Prose of an Army Psychiatrist

John,

Thanks for your support through the years at Walter Reed and Ft Bragg,

Best Cam

Nov 2010

Selected Major Works Written/Edited by the Author

*The Mental Health Response to the 9/11 Attack
on the Pentagon*

*Humanitarian Assistance and Health Diplomacy:
Military-Civilian Partnership in the 2004
Tsunami Aftermath*

*Mental Health and Mass Violence:
Evidence-Based Early Psychological Intervention
For Victims / Survivors of Mass Violence*

Combat and Operational Behavioral Health

Tearing Through the Moon:

Poems & Prose of an Army Psychiatrist

Elspeth Cameron Ritchie

THE WINEBERRY PRESS

Book design and production: Michael Register

Publisher: The Wineberry Press

Printed by Lightning Source USA

© 2010 Elspeth Cameron Ritchie

All rights reserved. No part of this book may be reproduced in any form or by any electronic or mechanical means (including photocopying, recording, or information storage and retrieval) without permission from the publisher and the author.

Library of Congress Cataloguing-in-Publication Data pending

Ritchie, Elspeth Cameron
    Tearing through the Moon: Poems and prose of an army psychiatrist

978-0-615-39710-8

The Wineberry Press
Washington DC

Acknowledgments
We wish to thank the editors in whose
journals these poems first appeared

"AIDS": *JAMA, Journal of the American Medical Association,* 1989;

"Arlington Cemetery", *Military Medicine*; 1990;

"Arlington Cemetery, Virginia": *JAMA, Journal of the American Medical Association,* 1996, *Uncharted Lines; Poems from the Journal of the American Medical Association,* editor Charlene Breedlove, American Medical Association, 1998;

"Electroconvulsive Therapy": *Electroconvulsive Therapy; The Journal of ECT*, 1993; *Blood and Bone, Poems by Physicians*, Angela Belli and Jack Coulehan, University of Iowa Press, 1998;

"Gun in the Closet"; *Journal of the American Academy of Child and Adolescent Psychiatry*, 1990/1991, *Primary Care; More Poems by Physicians,* editor Angela Belli and Jack Coulehan 2006;

"Flagstones"; *Life on the Line: Selections on Words and Healing,* editors, Sue Brannan Walker and Rosaly Demaios Roffman,: Negative Capability Press, Mobile, Alabama, 1992;

"Fireballs Inside the Pentagon"; *Military Medicine*, 2002;

"General Medical Officer, Camp Casey, Korea": *Military Medicine*, 1995;

"Hospital Spaces": *Washington Woman*, 1986; *Life on the Line: Selections on Words and Healing.* Editors Sue Brannan Walker & Rosaly Demaios Roffman,: Negative Capability Press, Mobile, Alabama, 1992; *On Doctoring*; editors Richard Reynolds and John Stone, Simon & Schuster, 1991, 1995, 2001;

"Infantryman—the DMZ, Korea": *Military Medicine*, 1992;

"Jewelweed": *Military Medicine*, 1991;

"Korean Birds, Yongsan Army Base, Seoul:" *JAMA, Journal of the American Medical Association,* 1996; *Uncharted Lines; Poems from the Journal of the American Medical Association*, editor Charlene Breedlove, American Medical Association, 1998;

"Language Barrier" *Washington Woman*, 1986; *Life on the Line: Selections on Words and Healing,* editors Sue Brannan Walker and Rosaly Demaios Roffman, Negative Capability Press, Mobile, Alabama, 1992, *On Doctoring*; editors Richard Reynolds and John Stone, Simon & Schuster 1991, 1995, 2001;

"Night Patrol, Mogadishu": *Mediphors* 1994;

"Nightshade Spell": *JAMA, Journal of the American Medical Association*, 1990;

"Notes on the Death of a Deer:" *Women and Death: 108 American Poets;* editors Jesse of the Genessee & Dorian Arana; © 1994 Grand Torpedo Press;

"On the Death of my Commanding General": *Military Medicine*, 1990;

"On the Ward": *Washington Woman,* 1986; *Life on the Line: Selections on Words and Healing,* editors Sue Brannan Walker and Rosaly Demaios Roffman,: Negative Capability Press, Mobile, Alabama, 1992, *On Doctoring*; editors Richard Reynolds and John Stone, Simon & Schuster, 1991, 1995, 2001;

"Pilot, Forty-Five, Desert Storm": *Military Medicine,* 1992;

"Paratrooper, Fort Bragg, North Carolina: *Military Medicine,* 1990;

"Pumpkin Flowers": *JAMA, Journal of the American Medical Association,* 1993, *Uncharted Lines; Poems from the Journal of the American Medical Association,* editor Charlene Breedlove, American Medical Association, 1998;

"Spring Lettuce": *Radcliffe Quarterly*, 1990, *Living in Storms,* Editor Thom Schramm, Eastern Washington University Press, 2008;

"Tearing Through the Moon", *JAMA, Journal of the American Medical Association*; 1990;

"The Dock": www.puddinghouse.com; 1992;

"The Intensive Care Unit, December 25, 1986"; *Washington Women*, 1986; *Life on the Line: Selections on Words and Healing,* editors Sue Brannan Walker and Rosaly Demaios Roffman,: Negative Capability Press, Mobile, Alabama, 1992; *On Doctoring*; editors Richard Reynolds and John Stone, Simon & Schuster, 1991, 1995, 2001;

"Washing Clothes, February 24, 1993, Mogadishu": *JAMA, Journal of the American Medical Association*, 1993.

*Dedicated to
My Children*

*Jessie Elspeth Curtis
Lyell Milford Curtis*

Contents

Author's Preface	17
Tearing Through the Moon	20
Arlington Cemetery I	22
AIDS	24
Arlington Cemetery II	26
On the Ward	28
The Intensive Care Unit	33
December 25, 1986	33
Language Barrier	36
Hospital Spaces	40
Gun in the Closet	43
Spring Lettuce	44
Paratrooper, Fort Bragg, North Carolina	46
Nightshade Spell	49
Flagstones	51
On the Death of My Commanding General	54
Electroconvulsive Therapy	58
Infantryman: DMZ, Korea	60
General Medical Officer, Camp Casey, Korea	63
Jewelweed	65
Pilot, Forty-Five, Desert Storm	66
Night Patrol, Mogadishu	68
Washing Clothes, February 24, 1993, Mogadishu	70
The Dock	74
Pumpkin Flowers	76
Notes on the Death of a Deer	78

Korean POW 80
Korean Birds 82
Fireballs Inside the Pentagon 85
Academic Conference in a Combat Zone 86
Black Uniform Ties 93
Ghosts of Abu Ghraib 94
Heart of Darkness: A Visit to Abu Ghraib 97
The Terrorist Tick 105
The Swan Feathers Castle 107
Army Surgeon, 2006 108
Detainee, Guantanamo Bay, Cuba 110
Army Medicine 112

Author's Preface

This slim volume is a distillation of 28 years of medicine. The poems are in chronological order, reflecting life as a medical student, intern, psychiatric resident, and then as an Army psychiatrist travelling to combat, conferences and military bases throughout the world.

The Army paid for medical school through the Health Professions Scholarship Program. The first poems were written as a medical student at George Washington University. The disease known now as AIDS was just surfacing, and several of the early poems, such as "AIDS" and "Tearing through the Moon," reflect those early years of uncertainty about the infectivity of the disease.

I trained as a psychiatry intern and resident at Walter Reed Army Medical Center. "On the Ward" was the first and only series for which I received a paycheck. The now defunct magazine *Washington Woman* paid me $1,500, with which I bought my first windsurfer. The series was later reprinted in *Life on the Line* and in *On Doctoring*. This early success prompted me to continue.

Most of my poetry has not been published in poetry magazines, but in technical journals, such as the *Journal of the American Medical Association, Military Medicine,* and even *Electroconvulsive Therapy*.

"Spring Lettuce" and "Electroconvulsive Therapy" are two of the poems written as a psychiatric resident. Like many others in the volume, they were an attempt to make sense of the deep unhappiness of many of my patients. "On the Death of my Commanding General" reflects real events and strong emotions about the death of General Jim Rumbaugh, an Army psychiatrist and wonderful man.

During residency I spent two weeks working with the Division Psychiatrist at Fort Bragg. "Paratrooper, Fort Bragg" grew out of that experience, which included talkingwith paratroopers and listening to their stories of girls, drinking and death.

After I completed my residency the Army assigned me to the Demilitarized Zone in Korea as the 2nd Infantry Division Psychiatrist. Four days after I arrived, Saddam invaded Kuwait. "General Medical Officer, Camp Casey" and "Pilot, 45, Desert Storm" are from that year.

Following that tour, I returned to Walter Reed, where I ran the inpatient ward. In the middle of that time, I deployed to Somalia. "Night Patrol, Mogadishu" and "Washing Clothes" date from that deployment. I returned to Walter Reed, completed a forensic psychiatry fellowship, then deployed again to Korea, where I ran the inpatient psychiatry unit at the 121st General Hospital in Seoul, Korea. "Korean Bird" and "Korean POW" grew out of that posting.

Then four more years at Walter Reed, followed by another four year stint at the Department of Defense's Health Affairs, working on mental health policy and women's health issues. I began to publish much more in the scientific literature, and wrote little poetry. "Fireballs Inside the Pentagon" was a single poem in a supplement to Military Medicine focusing on the 9/11 attacks on the Pentagon.

Thus during the period at Health Affairs and the last five years at the office of the Army Surgeon General, my focus has been on the wars in Iraq and Afghanistan, and helping Soldiers with the invisible wounds of war, including Post Traumatic Stress Disorders and Traumatic Brain Injury. I have also been asked to consult on the care of detainees in Guantanamo Bay and Iraq, and several of the poems and essays reflect that experience. Although I have been involved in other disasters, such as the 2006 tsunami in South East Asia and Hurricane Katrina, my work was operational, not poetic.

The death of Soldiers is another constant theme, reflected in the early poems "Arlington Cemetery," and in the later "Black Uniform Ties."

Despite all of these transitions, constants included the solace of working in the garden, both in Silver Spring and at Broomes Island, Maryland, where we also have a house. Thus many poems reflect garden and river themes.

My retirement date from the Army is September 30, 2010, and I want this book to capture these exciting and scary 28 years in Army medicine. Mine has been a great career, and one I always recommend to others.

Tearing Through the Moon

The hurricane rears:
clouds puff with anger,
shield stars from my red city.

Indoors, I interview
patients with AIDS.

Wind sucks at Washington streets,
licks skirts on flame-lipped girls,
gropes at monuments,
at crack houses, Congress.

I ask about lymph nodes,
risk factors, depression;
correlate results into papers,
pie charts, presentations.

My own dread roars,
tears at the moon.

My patients have slept with tainted men,
shot retrovirus in scarred veins,
breathed through diseased placentas.

They got trapped
in the henbane of desire.

Wrapped in leaves of death,
they watch for signs,
eat AZT, spray on pentamidine.

I too have been reckless,
roamed orange city streets,
kissed men in tight pants.

I too watch and fear,
insert IV's and start CPR.
After a handshake I wash.
Hands itch. I wash again.
I am no cold planet.
My palm trees bend.

The monsoon batters. Islands
of brittle coral sweep away.

My patients go out into the storm;
clouds blanket the inflamed moon.
Tears heat my skin.

Should I quit?
Stay behind locked doors?

No, I will live through the seasons.
That needle stick innocent—
my blood still tests negative.

Arlington Cemetery I

My brother and I mount our bikes,
ride December at a gallop across
Memorial Bridge, cement
our span of connections. Fords
honk. Cobbles crease our tires.

Visitor's Information maps Grandfather.
He led Russian cavalry at sixteen.
His saber hangs on my mother's wall,
beside my trophies from riding camp.
I rode hobbyhorse on his knee.
He taught me to shoot
at match sticks in the sand.

At the Tomb of the Unknowns
a private in dress blues, wool coat,
paces, snaps his rifle, paces.
Snowflakes tussle solemn air.
Tour buses snuffle the long hill.

General Lee's house nestles above
stone corps marching to the Potomac,
white on brown grass, buried wounds.
Soldiers from every war and time,
stilled infants, Army wives,
captains not thirty. Like me.
I too take the King's shilling.

Wind glues a green candy wrapper
to Grandfather's marker.

Decorated young colonel, incontinent old man
pinned by catheters in a nursing home,
he ate Twinkies, mind awry.

His brother, Ivan, was killed at nineteen,
fighting civil war in the Ukraine.
Ivan appeared in waking dreams.

Grandfather knew: time
to hang up saber and spurs.

At his funeral a dainty escort,
formal uniform and white gloves,
led Grandmother down the aisle.
Matching umbrellas hoisted to clouds.

Boots, reversed, on a black horse:
the caisson winds down to the grave.
Three last volleys. Taps.
The Old Guard folded the flag.

"What will you do with your life?"

My brother, his namesake, is silent.
We grow old, as yet without
combat or ribbons.

AIDS

My sperm encapsulates skulls.
My tears may kill.
Will I live to learn
if I've poisoned my new son?

The zoo of my body busted its gates.
Parasites burrow my open lungs,
the virus inches through my nerves.
Cancer blotches my skin. Purple
boils erupt. I am Job.

Yet, it was a night
sweet as Cleopatra's asp,
his skin a camellia.
We courted like crowned cranes,
frolicked like sea lions, howled as caged wolves.

If he were not dead, would I hate him?

My sight strobes in decreasing shades of pale.
My mind lies beige, limp, sticky.
When the doctor asks, I pretend to subtract.

Friends venture toward my infected bed.
They do not touch my blotched hand.
My wife used to love me. Now,
she enters in yellow gown and gloves.
My mother fears my drool.

I smell the hospital shop carnations.

I would like to sweep in a green rotten canoe
toward the Atlantic,
drown in peace.
Salt grass would hug my empty skin.

In the hospital buzzing with white coats
bugs swarm in my lungs.
Asleep I drown, awake I gasp.

A catfish stranded,
I wait for needles
and creeping snake death.

Where is the garden?

Arlington Cemetery II

General Lee's garden:
purple shoots rise;
jackets open, kids
race down the paths;
tombstones settle in
snow melt and March wind.

Stone crosses parade the slopes:
soldiers fallen in battle
or faded in nursing homes.
Snow highlights graves
with translucent peace.

Kennedy's eternal flame,
fire blue and gold,
burns flanked by cameras.

Tall soldiers with shined brass
stamp, black shoes click heels,
change arms, honor a rock box,
Tomb of the Unknown Soldier.
Skulls and arm bones tumble,
souls riding the gusts.

We tromp to the ridge
where physician soldiers lie,
surveying the Potomac.

Walter Reed rests here,
"Conqueror of Yellow Fever,"
enabler of the Panama Canal.

General Rumbaugh died
parachuting into Honduras,
airdropping a hospital.

I remember: bugles calling Taps,
sharp rifle cracks,
the long line of mourners.

His epitaph: "He did not
merely exist in our world;
he roared through it, carrying
the rest of us in his vortex."

The breeze blows, flags snap.
So many grieve here.

Next, we seek my grandfather:
small headstone with Russian
cross. He fought in three wars,
and died at 85, demented.
No tourists.

Daffodils spurt upwards.
More bugles sound,
trees dream of bloom.

On the Ward

I carry three AIDS patients, about the same as any other intern on the medicine service at my hospital. One is a young black male, one a young white female, the third a middle-aged black male. The young man received a lethal blood transfusion three years ago. The black man, married with children, has told us of his homosexual activity. The white female has known no risk factors, but we suspect IV drug use. She may simply have slept with an infected man.

A scant two years ago, in a hospital that has a high proportion of AIDS patients, an intern would average only one AIDS patient. I was a third-year medical student then. I cared for, and became close to, my intern's AIDS patient.

His name was Dave. He was attractive, very thin, and gay. He ran fevers and we could not find the cause. So we drew culture every night, seeking he bug that shot his temperature up to 104 degrees. He would ask me late at night, while I was setting up the tubes and bottles, why I was planning to hurt him. I never had an answer I believed in. The blood cultures were always negative. We finally treated for pneumocystis pneumonia. Then he spiked fevers in reaction to the antibiotic.

At first I gowned and gloved whenever I entered his room; I hated to draw his blood, fearing needle sticks and contamination. I grew more relaxed; sometimes I almost forgot to put on gloves when I drew blood cultures.

He hated being in the hospital. He could not eat the food and seemed thinner every day. I tried once bringing him his favorite flavor of ice cream, butter pecan, from the cafeteria. He thanked me for it but I think he just let it melt.

I rotated off service. I remember his fantasies of leaving, going home to Florida, and floating downstream in a leaky canoe. I'm sure he is long since dead.

Now, with so many patients to care for, both tragedy and precautions are routine. Any patient is risky. I recently stuck myself with a needle for the first time in my life. Fortunately, the married lady had no risk factors. I sent off hepatitis screen and HTLV-3 (now called HIV) tests anyway. They are due back in two weeks. Should I sleep with my husband until then?

All of my HIV patients are sick, hurting, up here on the medicine ward. Asymptomatic ones wait for disposition on the self-care ward. They also wait for the first signs of real illness: the white thrush over the throat, the purple spots of Kaposi's, and shortness of breath of pneumocystis.

My middle-aged black man will die soon. He has cryptococcal meningitis and pneumocystis pneumonia. The titer of cryptococcus is the highest that this hospital has ever seen. Recently he had become even more short of breath and his tremor has gotten worse. He also has painful rectal herpes. Today his bronchoscopy specimens show an acid-fast bacilli, probably a special form of tuberculosis that immunosuppressed patients get. He is already on four toxic antibiotics. What do we do now?

He finally allowed me to tell his family that he is very sick. They do not know of his AIDS diagnosis. His numerous and respectable family arrived last week. They questioned me as to whether he has cancer. I hedge and talk of his pneumonia. They ask me whether he will come home soon. Not yet, he's very sick, I answer. They suspect the truth, I think, but do not ask. His wife has not called.

Interns see a lot of sickness and death. We build up protective mechanisms: she was old, he drank too much. If somebody our age is dying, our mental dams break away. It could be my best friend (who is gay), it could be my college-age brother, (who is not). There, but for the grace of God, go I.

My young black male received a blood transfusion after a minor accident two years ago. He developed a painful throat ulcer and fevers. He was diagnosed six months ago. He did not tell his family for three more months. He comes from a remote town in Kentucky and he did not know how his family would respond. They are angry that he did not tell them sooner. He is about to go home for a convalescent leave. What will his neighbors say? Will they believe the blood transfusion or suspect his morals? Will anybody enter the house?

He is still attractive and personable, if thin. This morning he told me how nice I looked. I replaced his feeding tube; his throat hurts too much to swallow. We are doctor and patient. Two years ago I would have hoped that he would ask me out.

I tell myself severely that it is no good crying for him. He has five sisters who will weep. I have other patients to care for.

The third patient, the young white female, is hostile, remote. She has end-stage renal disease and is on dialysis. You have to coax her into drawing her blood. I don't want to do it either, but the consultants recommend an antibiotic level. Of course, they are not the ones who stick her. I am her intern.

I have others patients, patients with heart, lung, liver, and kidney disease, but they come and go quickly. They die or leave. Except, of course, the elderly waiting for nursing home placement. I hope to send one to a home soon. He has been in the hospital for ninety days.

I also care for healthy HIV-3 positive patients. They are still working and active and only come to the hospital for staging. While here, they have their blood drawn for T-cell count and their skin pricked to see if they react to allergens. Then they return home. Some to their jobs and families. One recent twenty-nine-year-old admission was diagnosed eight months ago. His wife was initially negative; a month ago she converted. They have two children, six and eight, who have not yet been tested.

In a year or three, they will probably be lying in a hospital bed with pneumocystis and cryptococcus raging through their brains and bodies.

Fortunately I am HIV negative. I feel lucky. My husband cooks me supper when I surface after call. My older brother and his wife just had a healthy baby. I know infected two-year-olds.

I warn my younger unmarried brother. My friends all question me. I have only moralistic-sounding statements to make. Don't sleep around!— even occasionally. I am glad that I am married and tested negative twice. If I were single, would I insist on a blood test before sleeping with a man? I hate to sound so pessimistic when friends grill me at a cocktail party—but I don't want my friends to die that kind of death.

I wish the families of AIDS patients would come more often. You won't catch it by persuading them to eat! They need their mothers, wives, sons here. They are hurt, sick, dying. They need family. I substitute where I can. It is too little for them and too painful for me.

The Intensive Care Unit
December 25, 1986

The lady lies
surrounded by a court
of alarmed machines.
They record life:
blood pressure, pulse
and respirations.
The lady does not talk
so we read her numbers:
the language of
her failing heart.

Her daughter questions
incessantly,
her husband is mute.
Grandchildren in the waiting room
watch Roadrunner.
Over the thickest of IV poles
nurses snatch glimpses
of M*A*S*H and St. Elsewhere.
Electronic Christmas carols
spew over her bed.

Once she ate, excused herself
to her powder room, breathed on her own.
Now, her body is helpless
and her mind.
Perhaps her soul
wonders at her ruined holiday.
She did not mail her Christmas cards.

I draw the bloods,
apologize for sticking her again.
She does not twitch.
Only the ventilator answers.
The Redskins' field goal
should excite her to wake.
Instead her heart throws a
crazy beat.
Then another—
time for another EKG.

I sigh; no sleep again
tonight, Christmas night.
I nibble microwave popcorn and
stale fruitcake, swig Diet Coke.
A tube bears Osmolyte for her.

The clouded moon through the window
over her busy bed, reminds me
of when I believed in Angels.
Every Christmas, when I was a child,
I searched the orange city skies
for their shining.

I seek again tonight.
No answer.
Winged men triumphantly
should bear her soul to Heaven,
bring me a festival stocking.

Yet, I hope she does not die today
(though my tasks would be fewer).
Her grandchildren should not remember

Christ's birthday and new toys
by her death.

Her blood pressure is dropping.

I will try to keep her breathing until tomorrow.

Language Barrier

It gets hard to communicate in the old language.

When I started medical school, our courses were basically word lists. The lists were anatomy and microbiology. We memorized the eleven muscles of the thumb, chambers of the heart, classification of diseases of the colon. It was like studying French. All those nouns to memorize!

We all studied how the organs work, of course: the lungs exchange gases, the heart spins blood around, the kidney filters the waste. We peered at purple-painted bacteria, watched antibiotics scour those bugs from the petri dishes. But it was the names that we were tested on, the vocabulary that would isolate us as physicians.

In medical school we were taught never to refer to patients as a disease. To say, "the gall bladder down the hall," was demeaning. We resolved always to give our patients due respect.

Back in those pre-war days, they also warned us to continue to communicate with our families, friends, and children. "Spend an hour with your child every day." "Take time out to go running." "It's important to keep up with politics."

Then came third year, the clinical years. The dicta were moot. Even if we had a free half hour it was more important, it seemed, to polish up the history and physical for presentation to our preceptors, to volunteer to hold retractors for another cholestectomy, to scour the library for articles on esoteric aspects of lupus.

Shakespeare, botany, evolution were lost fantasies. Once, I learned how many petals adorn roses. Now, flower petals are submerged beneath liver enzymes.

The gap widened. How could our husbands know the frustrations of missing a blood draw three times, then have the intern draw pints with ease? When eating with in-laws we could not talk at dinner of the smell of melena (old blood leaking out of the rectum), nor of the skin lesions on our AIDS patients.

As time rolled by, life outside the hospital dwindles. Now I am an intern.

"How as your day, dear?" I politely inquire at home at eight p.m. after a night on call.

"Terrible. The computer went down on a very important project. I was at work from eight this morning to seven tonight. Then the bus broke down. I need a drink. Oh, yes, how was yours?"

I am silent for a minute. "Well, I was lucky last night on call. I slept from one a.m. to four a.m. Then I got a drunk hit from the nursing home with chest pain. But I slept again from six-thirty to seven-thirty. So, almost four hours.

Of course that is in a cell-like call room in the bottom of a creaky bunk bed. Meal carts creaking and nurses gossiping loudly outside. Another thirty-seven-hour shift. But I got close to four hours. These days that's cause for celebration. Almost."

So, my sympathies for others' trials are slight. Unfairly, I become impatient with their tribulations. Sometimes I explode.

"Don't tell me about your difficulties with your computer. My favorite patient is dying. And one of my AIDS patients developed pneumocystis pneumonia. And you're whining because you partied too late with friends when I was on call and only got six hours of sleep."

Non-medical friends sympathize. "Oh, you poor dear." They try to help and are puzzled when I am nasty and irritable.

In cocktail conversations acquaintances say: "That's a terrible system. It should not be allowed. I wouldn't want to be cared for by somebody who had been up all night." Noses tilt. Their anger descends on me. I'm a doctor.

Thanks. I don't want to care for them either after I've been up all night. But I can't afford the energy to waste on rage at the system.

After all, it's a privilege to be a doctor.

My fellows on the battlefront become my in-arms comrades at least until we rotate into a new service. We joke about the drunk hit. We share doughnuts and popcorn. On rounds we talk about the gall bladder down the hall and the valve in Room 4116.

We develop sexual fantasies about those in the trenches with us. At two a.m. your resident is your staff. When a patient is spurting blood out of his tracheostomy and you together insert a central line (an IV in the neck), transfer him to the unit, and save his life (at least for now), then you are brothers. Afterwards you raise Diet Cokes in companionship.

How can your husband compare to him, the man who just helped you save a life? Marriages are made in medical school and dissolve in internship.

But the deans who pontificated in medical school about the values of outside interests were right. We—the battered products of medical school—know that to be true. It just gets harder. The gap widens.

"She didn't make it. We coded her and shocked her and put a pacemaker into her. It didn't work. Why, I'm not sure. We asked for an autopsy. What should we have for dinner?"

Hospital Spaces

Life is defined by bounds:
here, sickness and health are also sequestered.
We have the isolated rooms of infection,
and social wards of men whose
efforts are limited by chest pain.
They play spades with vigor.

Metal rails surround the beds with
air bubbling up through fluid plastic beads,
confining and relieving the comatose.

The staff has large hectic rooms
with multiple desks and phones ringing.
We report local recoveries and deaths,
call the public health department,
and field calls about AIDS and angina.

Chairs are constantly swiped from one desk
to another, as an intern dashes in to scribble a note, feet hurting,
or tries to turf a patient to a nursing home.
This one has been in for ninety-seven days.

The hallways link the separate worlds.
Like salt sea barnacles
groups of doctors cling on the walls,
discussing their patients' potassium
(barely out of earshot),
drinking instant coffee, grateful
if a stretcher appears to perch on.
Two hours sleep last night.
A long day's journey ahead.

The pantry is guarded by fierce ladies
microwaving the trays of hospital food.
Medical students sneak in to steal
leftover chocolate pudding.

Elevators frustrate. Waiting,
pondering my clipboard,
I can hear them ping at every floor.
Rumbling food racks are loaded.
To the lab, to x-ray, then to surgery clinic,
to drop off another consult.
I wave to friends on contralateral trips.
How many romance start, and stop,
with the opening and shutting of doors?

Sometimes a patient crashes on
the seventh floor.
With cardiac monitor beeping,
and code drugs on the stretcher,
in case his heart stops,
we transport a patient vomiting blood
to the ICU on the fourth floor,
squeezing past the linen carts
in the narrow hallways,
hoping that we will make it,
before he stops breathing.

So far, so good.

More lines intersect.
The snack bar, the chapel, and barber shop,
the clinics and the morgue.
The library offers a soft chair for sleep.

My beeper is a leash,
jerking me back
to headaches and chest pain.

When I finally break out
into the winter evening,
after 38 hours of the hospital,
it is amazing that
I can remember where the car is,
and that yellow crocuses
are blooming.

Gun in the Closet

Mom hates it when Dad
cleans the barrel,
then aims his sights at
Aunt Jenn on the wall.

Can't study any more. Instead
I play "Guns and Roses."
Dad's gone to Saudi.

Mom's at the bar with that man.
I wait at home alone.

The liquor cabinet
only holds Dubonnet now.
I drank the sherry.

The red paint in my bedroom
blisters lonely walls.
No one noticed that knife.

My dog was run over last week.
Mom said, "Anyway, he drooled."

I tried aspirin last week
after Tom laughed "No" to the dance.
It only made me vomit.

The house is silent.
Dad taught me how to shoot.

Mom's still not home.

Spring Lettuce

When the March wind tossed sandy Maryland,
when the osprey began to dive for sticks,
when jellyfish floated in, their wombs red,
we planted the first black seeds.

The city was closed, rain leashing
the hospital in tethers of traffic.
Patients played cards, smoked, dreamed.
I stayed late, dictating charts.

Radishes burst first, tearing up to the sun.
Timidly the lettuce peeked to spy on
the fanfarewell of the geese, and duck
at shotgun shells raking from dead blinds.

Many men and women flew in from Europe,
lashed to gurneys, legs twitching,
minds aswarm, families left, souls beaten.
We helped them up, switched their meds.

Time to plant feathery dill and fetid cilantro,
but the purple basil failed of cold.
Starflowers thrust through the antique grass.
Tractors flung the furrows wide.

A man put a plastic bag over his head and died
in a froth of vomit. We could not revive him.
Police came. Cameras flashed.
Patients cried. I clamped down. Work to do.
White and red radishes fill the fridge.
Time for tomatoes, tamped down with dung.
Tears finally came, as the cages went

around the stalks. How could you suicide in spring?

The inquest ended. No negligence.
Patients found their clothes, called their wives.
Volleyballs pounded the office windows.
A nurse announced. Baby showers.

Now the ospreys tend their eggs
in the locust leaning over the tide.
Underneath sound the thwocks of croquet balls,
we dug the sailboat from the sand.

A woman with AIDS lost her unborn child.

She asked me whether he would go to heaven
or hell, since he was tainted. I replied,
"Heaven, I think." She, too, wants to die.

A hundred head of lettuce extrude.
Spinach has gone to seed. Girls glide
on the beach. I read Freud.
Black men plant tobacco by hand.

Time for me to leave the ward.
Cocaine addicts revolve through the doors.
I feed the staff bread and lettuce.
Turkey vultures roost in the barn.

The baby jellyfish gather offshore.
Boundaries of ward and garden fade.
Worms swam in both. I weed and fertilize.
Sails fly, frantically, through the river.

Paratrooper, Fort Bragg, North Carolina

I am lonely and cold.
Nor wartime. No Vietnam.
Peacetime is empty here
in Fayetteville, home of The Airborne.

If only I could parachute in
somewhere real. Fight with my unit.
Get my combat badge, be a hero.
Make Mom be proud, stop drinking.

Instead we rehearse how to land,
Shiver in the November cold
of pine-ridden North Carolina.
Will I break my leg tonight?

Two C-130's crouch on the strip.
Two hours more until we board.
A message from my current girl
tacked on the barracks door.

Can't call till we're back
in the dawn. Is it "Dear John"?
Is she pregnant? Or broke?
Do I care? Not tonight.

My father, a colonel,
jumped until he crashed
into a camouflaged jeep.
Now a wheelchair is home.

My mother switched to vodka then,
my brother went to med school,

I ran off to jump school.
On weekends I also drink.

I pack my chute, tighten straps.
This year three jumpers died.
I'm out of smokes. Bum one.
What are lungs compared to legs?

My squad buddies have wives.
They fight. Babies squall.
I just want a woman.
Tomorrow night, it's Bottom's Up.

Women there don't wed.
Dollar bills fly instead.
My roommate bedded a dancer.
Two shots cured him.

My doctor brother is staid.
Disapproves of cigarettes,
and me. He hasn't jumped.
Coward. Do you love me?

I try so hard to match
you and Dad. I've quit cocaine,
Won my stripes. I jump.
What else makes a man? My M-16?

Time to load. We file aboard
in order. The plane is cold.
I clip to the static line.
Dad's voice calls to me.

I cannot hear him
with the gibbering wind
in my ears. The jumpmaster
calls, "Jump!" I do.

Nightshade Spell

I will concoct a brew, witches' stew,
nightshade, henbane, mandrake root,
swirl it with a spoon of horn,
to make you stay in love with me.

I poach your eggs and bake your bread,
yet you will turn and go away.
I plant your seed and rub your head.
Will you stay in love with me?

Were I a witch, with perfect pitch,
I could enchant you easily.
No need for lipstick or cocaine;
herbs would fasten you to me.

I will wait till summer's wane
to cast a spell, a binding shell.
I will dance beneath hemlock trees,
draw the October moon to me.

Nightshade is the drug of Circe,
enchantress of the isle.
She stole men's minds, made them swine,
but could not keep Ulysses.

Henbane is the devil's eye.
Eat henbane and you will fly
over the lake of the country side,
light fires on the moonlit tide.

Yank a mandrake from the ground.
Whirl thirty times around.
Drop powder in your man's drink;
you will govern what he thinks.

I put perfume in my brown hair,
nutmeg, basil in my bread.
Can I hold your dreaming soul?
Will you keep me in your head?

Flagstones

Time to plant new bulbs
in my family's backyard.
Last year's bulbs grew bloodless shoots,
drooped to earth, no tulips.

Days shorten, October ends.
My father made this garden
thirty years ago,
laid flagstones in the shade
of the tulip magnolia
where even lilies wouldn't grow.

Stream splits flat from hill.
M brother and I trapped crayfish here.
My mother laughed, offered them for dinner.
We ate poached eggs instead.

Now the water is caught
on bricks and leaves.
Now my parents are divorced.

A creased brown photograph is taped
in my grandfather's nursing home.
Framed by a stockade fence,
a small girl thrusts an ice cream cone,
vanilla on her pout.

I ease my mother's father into his chair,
roll him to the sea of meals,
pat his face free of pudding,
remember I am that girl.

Last year, my husband tore down the stockade,
snapped old rails against his knees.
A backhoe dug new foundations
cracked across lilies and flagstones.

The tulip tree died, roots severed.
Concrete and cigarettes block
the muddy paths of worms
Yellow tinges the azaleas.

I dig anyway, time to plant,
bags of topsoil and bulb food,
iris and daffodils waiting.

The shovel rings on rock.
I strain to pry it up.
My pitchfork outlines, then
levers up a buried flagstone.

My father's flagstones,
bedrock for picnics and jump ropes,
are buried by construction and time.
New growth is blocked.

Again metal clangs slate.
A bed of stone lies six inches deep,
Covered with earth and last year's bulbs;
their roots spread out instead of down.

My grandfather is dying,
my father remarried,
my mother traps poetry,
my brother teaches his son to fish.

I pile up the old stones,
mix in the new dirt,
throw exposed worms back,
plant thirty narcissus bulbs
and clumps of snowdrops.

On the Death of My Commanding General

Shocked. Cold. Lonely.
1:30 a.m., March 9th.
On call tonight when
a ward tech spread the news.

General Rumbaugh is dead.
Not official yet.
Jump accident in Honduras.

C-130 coming down the strip.
Hard core medic gonna to take a little trip.

Our general dead? No.
Last week, he walked these long halls.
Sunset outlined the brick spires
of the old hospital,
as he talked of plans for Walter Reed.

He jumped from a plane, stood up,
went to work, developed flank pain.
Coded on the way to Texas.
Doctors battled to keep him.

How could we lose this fight?

I call my chief at home,
his friend of twenty years.
I cry, not official yet.

Get up, buckle up, shuffle to the door.
Jump right out and count to four.

A charge nurse weeps as she charts,
recalls his bushy mustache
when he was a resident here,
a psychiatry resident, like me.

Corridors creep cold and vacant.
Patients are asleep, unknowing.
My calls made, I lie in the call room,
on a plastic mattress.
A moon outlines uncaring Washington.

I'm here to help others.
I'm the psychiatrist on duty.

But if asked to comfort
will I break down instead?

A welcome page calls me
to high blood pressure.
Later, 3:30 a.m., chapel empty
I ask why.

He had four children, a wife.
I'd wished he were my father.

Light breaks on Walter Reed
and the half-masted flag.
I break the news again.
Many now to weep, hold tight hands.

If my main don't open wide.
I got another one by my side.

He was our commander.
How could he leave us?
He was too old to jump.
No one could stop General Jim.

He wanted to land with
the 82nd Airborne, his old command.
He would have been fifty March l6th.
Next surgeon general, we thought.

Jim played tennis in March dawn
carrying a phone to call the Pentagon.
His son biked by to watch him serve.
Nice shot, Dad.

If my main should fail me too,
Watch out below. I'm coming through.

The soldier doctor was pinned
with his second star last fall.
His family was so proud.
He didn't change. Still "Jim."

No more laughing, smashing
the ball into the net?
Surely he will swing by the wards,
curing and caring and hoping for
parking garages for his new command.

I imagine his cadence still,
see him jogging towards Rock Creek
in a Mickey Mouse sweatshirt,
fresh dreams upon his back.

*If my main should fail me too,
bury me in my dress blues.*

Electroconvulsive Therapy

This motor won't start.

My mate takes me
to the hospital, again.
Why? Drugs don't work.
My mouth is dry, bowels
clogged, brain slow,
singed heart falters.
Life is shot.

I wish I could fade
into a junkyard,
with other carcasses of colonels and cars.

Electricity, doctors insist.
They want to jump-start me.
They should give up,
hang up their cables,
like the noose I dream of.

How can a seizure help?
Again wife and daughters plead.
We are destined to failure;
I finally yield.

They wheel me down,
put a plastic mask on
my face, drugs in weakened
veins. I smell apples.

Four more times: dreams
of stockcars and winning,
and, they say, convulsions.

The scent of fruit, and
the buzz of honeybees
return to me.

My brain begins to rev,
the starter motor works;
we used to neck in my T-bird.
I feel my sex jumping.

Infantryman: DMZ, Korea

Flame blue dress, black hair
Too slim waist, spike heels.
A case of OB beer. Wrapped
in my poncho, I dream.

Pre-dawn, réveille;
Platoon sergeant yells.
My toes are ice.
I pull on boots,
Kevlar, M-16,
lie on the snow for
stand-to, point my
weapon at North Korea,
ponder girls and chow.

Bacon, eggs, weak coffee.
For lunch, an MRE.
Seven more nights of
churned mud. Once more,
no mail from home.

Shouts. A trac flipped,
crushing the head of
the leader of my squad.

In memoriam:
three stacked rifles,
capped by his helmet,
boots shined blacker
than he ever wore.

In dreary formation,
our sergeant calls roll.
Silence echoes his name.

He played third base,
would overthrow the ball
to me on first. I cursed him
last week when we lost.
Now taps.
I have his lucky mitt—

he courted his wife at
high school games—
and his March Playboy.
I seek our chaplain,
what should I do?
Send the mitt to his son,
throw away the porn.

Instead, in garrison,
I lie on my bunk,
with the magazine,
pop a beer,
peer at white skin,
forever glossy
gleaming legs.

Our picture was in
The Indianhead,
as we learned to move,
shoot and communicate.
Grainy black and white.

He sent copies home.
I brought my girl a paper.
She works at The Liberty Club.
We Texas two-stepped,
drank, made love.
Twenty thousand won.
Cheap to be a man.

Tonight, she doesn't come.
An officer?
I try to phone home:
all trunks are busy.
Country music wails
of loss and coffins.

How will I survive
training, lust, war,
my loneliness here?

The chaplain cannot answer,
for I dare not ask.

General Medical Officer, Camp Casey, Korea

Saturday, the PX is filled;
soldiers eat Anthony's pizza,
buy videos and lacquer boxes
for pregnant wives back home.

I ride to the East Casey gym,
pump iron, admire my growing arms,
compete with younger men and
wipe sweat from the vinyl bench.

Later the officer group goes
to the Second to None club
where a Korean dancer writhes
wearily to Credence Clearwater.

The men too are bored, waiting for
the trip to downrange, outside the gate.
There older women with flat faces
squat on the curb, pimping for
minishorted girls in the alleys.

Stalls line the road, sell soju,
fried squid and 2 ID t-shirts.
Venders bargain with five fingers,
deaf since rubella-shrouded birth.

Shattering fantasy, a siren shrills.
Soldiers leave drinking, run to barracks,
throw on BDUs, lace combat boots,
brush teeth, race to the weapons room.

They leave with M-16s, gas masks,
rucksacks, MOPP gear, candy bars,
to service HUM-Vs in the motor pool.

We doctors, useless, play cards,
or sleepwith rucks for pillows.
The work here is for fighting men
whose job is to train and wait.
Our job is to support and repair
broken heads, penile drips,
wrists slashed, men wanting home.

3:30 AM, alert over, we check our 45s.
But my beeper sounds: a man jumped
off the roof of his hooch. Soju
again. Sweet potato liquor.
I medevac him to Seoul.

Now dawn. Yellow lights still
outline the misted motor pool.
Faint rain hides tanks, quonset huts,
wreathes mountains which float to
North Korea. Our enemy seems remote.

Yet students throw firebombs.
There is movement north of the DMZ,
tanks clog the country roads,
and a crazy man overran Kuwait.

We also wait, drink OB beer,
sometimes pray, fear and
wish for Saudi sand and war.
We pass the time betting.

Jewelweed

Hollow stems overstep my garden.
Weeds shade out begonias, lily bells.
Forgotten since their manic birth
pansies stretch weak stems,
velvet hearts arch towards shielded sun.

I yank out jewelweed.
Dirt embraces roots,
but resistance is weak.
The grass is tougher,
leaving foxholes where
a tattered mouse lies,
my cat's tribute abandoned.

This final weeding comes too soon.
I will be transplanted from summer
to the Cold War, Korea,
where tanks festoon gardens of graves,
guns overhand foreign flowers,
cooks serve dogs for lunch.

To pull up friendship is the hardest.
Some goodbyes are soft pops,
scars smoothed by rain.
Leaf bags line by time's curb.

Now my hoe catches on brambles.
Blackberry thorns
snag my heart as I leave,
and etch your name.

Pilot, Forty-Five, Desert Storm

Christmas. 1968:
I flew Hueys which
spat red fire balls
at smoky rice paddles,
armor beneath my feet.

Charlie answered in green,
tracing a Noel ballet,
dancing me to the hottest
landing zones, to exchange
gifts of bullets for the dead.

January cold, 1991:
I calculate the costs
at my chipped metal desk.
My shoulders sport eagles,
but my wings are frayed.

Younger men fly the birds
which rocket bunkers full
of Arabs faint with thirst.
Discordant they fire up,
erupt and die.

My bride, pregnant when
I deployed to Vietnam,
is again stout. My baby
now flirts with pilots,
in tight flight suits.
Buttocks and chests taut,
they coo and flex arms,
as I once did.

I still fly, but not
Apaches. I know older birds:
Blackhawks, Scouts,
blades of other wars.

Last week my buddy's helicopter
crashed in a corn field.
(He pulled me from a wreck in Nam—
for ten days we ate jungle worms
and at last broke through
rain forest to the beach.)
Taps, yet again.

Sometimes, fatigue clouds
my sight and I hide
tremors in my hands.
Ahead: retirement.

When I die, I want to
soar with my steel eagles
and rise on melting wings
into a sun without wars,
a fireball that never ages.

Night Patrol, Mogadishu

Glass splinters spark
from the horned quarter moon;
lighted shards are a sharpened
glow worms on the wall,
humping the dark concrete.

We Marines file, boots
crunching rocks and
bones, kicking trash and
tossed wooden legs.

Streets open gaped mouths
to men with teeth
of rust and bullets.

A serape spins us to point fangs and guns
at a shattered door.
Only an old woman.

Females are born antique
in modern Somalia.
Festered men just
kill, and die, young.

Death shines here,
not age.

A round caught Ben Sunday,
cracked his helmet.
His body went home.

Silence now. We inch on.
CNN flashed skeletal limbs.
Now Mogadishu arms have meat
and sling shit and stones.

I want to shoot;
but the priest lectured
hell is for
those who kill.
My sergeant got nailed
for throwing back a rock.

Too many thoughts!
I have to focus,
listen and watch
for a flash, a spear,
the burst of a mine.

None here to minister;
fear grabs the sticky bottom
of my soul.

A click, an oiled bolt?
I turn, squeeze my rifle.

The night explodes
into fire scorpions,
turning the moon
to blood and black.

Washing Clothes, February 24, 1993, Mogadishu

There's always laundry.

We are locked down today—the first day of Ramadan—because of the riots. The Somalis are burning tires and pelting military vehicles with rocks. Small-arms and crew-served weapons fire has permeated the morning.

All non-mission-essential travel has been curtailed. I don't bother even to mention to my boss the follow-up visits I want to make to the soldiers and marines in the nearby compounds—I know what his response would be to any suggestion of leaving the relatively secure university area for the roadblocks erected by angry Somalis.

I know too that he would be right. Nevertheless, I chafe at the confinement.

I am a psychiatrist. Normally I have a hospital-based practice at a US Army medical center. I usually drive my aged Honda to morning staff meetings, wear a polyester uniform shirt and skirt on the job, and putter in the vegetable garden of my suburban home after work. Normally, I use a washing machine.

Today I wear a DCU (desert camouflage uniform). I remove my shoulder holster—with its 9-mm pistol—to type, as it rubs my back wrong. The magazine, with ten bullets, is in my large cargo pocket.

I had loaded the magazine in the weapon earlier today, when the gunfire started. We crouched in the hallway of the university building for 30 minutes, flak jackets and helmets on, helicopters wheeling over head. Finally, the all clear came, the other soldiers returned to the battalion aid station, and I went back to washing my uniforms.

It's amazing how fast dirty clothes accumulate when it is 100 degrees, the grit and sand blow constantly, and you have to wash them by hand. Only three days' worth, but that means six T-shirts, one set of the heavy DCUs, six pairs of underwear, 12 socks, and a few loose towels, running shorts, and Odor-Eaters.

I could give the garments to the Somali laundry. The tall, graceful, brightly scarved women look lovely as they scrub. But these brown T-shirts all look alike, and sometimes they are switched or lost. My very cool Swedish Field Hospital T-shirt (a swap with a Swedish pediatrician for an army shirt) might disappear. But with the riots, I doubt our launderers will be able to travel here tomorrow.

So I haul five-gallon jugs from the water tank (known also as the "water buffalo"), pour tepid water into smaller buckets, and throw in some detergent and the socks. The water immediately turns brown.

I wash my own clothes too because there is little else to do here. One of the many problems with being in a medical unit in tactical situation is that there often is not much with which to entertain oneself. Ample medical assets must always be available, in case a helicopter crashes or a truck flips over or soldiers are shot. In Bardera, a month ago, we were busy with many soldiers who came sick—with malaria and dengue fever, we discovered. But much of the time the medics sit around, treating an occasional ankle sprain or bug bite, or playing Game Boy.

Like my vehicle and my uniform, my job here is different than it was in the States. I am part of the 528th Combat Stress

Control Detachment, a small group of psychiatrists, social workers, and behavioral science technicians. Our task is to provide front-line mental health intervention.

So we navigate Mogadishu's streets in our army pickup trucks visiting different units and battalion aid stations. We live in a network of compounds, using concertina wire, walls topped with glass shards, and armed guards in towers to deter thieves, bandits, and small boys. The children often manage to slip in anyway, rummaging through our trash for discarded MREs (meals ready to eats).

I got my military driver's license before I left Fort Bragg. Back in the States, officers seldom drive military vehicles. Here I usually drive, since I only carry a pistol. A long wooden tent peg lies in my lap, to fend off the reaching hands of the locals. Sitting in the back of the truck, the enlisted men, with their M16s, function as "air guards"—to return fire in case we are shot at. We do "Mogadishu rounds," driving to the stadium where the marines live, negotiating potholed streets to the 86th Evacuation Hospital, and weathering fire fights on our way to transportation units.

We have worked with marine units that took casualties, with truck drivers who inadvertently killed Somali kids who ran under their wheels, and with military police who were hit with rocks and even shot at but were not allowed to shoot back. We try to handle any psychological sequelae before the soldiers have problems severe enough for them to become psychiatric patients.

The demand for our services has been relatively light. Before we came here, we expected to treat soldiers with "famine fatigue" from seeing desperately sick children or rotting corpses. But very few service members have actually seen starving or dying Somalis. Instead, the stressors are similar to those of low-intensity guerrilla warfare, with an erratic host population accustomed to years of civil war. The people may thank you, demand water or MREs, or shoot at you.

A bandit killed a relief worker two days ago, for no clear reason. I met the rest of her organization's group yesterday. They stood huddled on the airfield tarmac, watching after the C-141 that carried her body home. We were introduced by the civil affairs officers, who had helped to arrange security for the relief organizations. Obviously, the security had not worked. The relief group was not angry at the military but rather sad and puzzled about the shooting of a young woman who was bringing in food.

I had hoped to do a critical stress incident debriefing with them, as we had done with our soldiers who took casualties. My chain of command says it is too dangerous to go out the front gate. Maybe Friday, if the demonstrations let us, he informed me. I am frustrated, but I understand.

So, like the other medical personnel, I wait. The makeshift gym is busy right now. The newest paper is a week old, does not mention Somalia, and I have already read it twice. But, fortunately, it is time to rinse out my T-shirts and hang my socks on the line. Yes, the clothes will quickly get dusty with all the blowing sand. But doing laundry may prevent this psychiatrist from going stir-crazy.

After that I'll clean my weapon.

The Dock

Pilings and boards create
a crossing over our river
which merges fresh and salt.

From the dock we toss stale
basil bread to swans:
the young with brown trim,
parents with unfurled wings
like feathered scrolls.

Seagulls, greedy beggars,
scold me and dive
for sinking crumbs.
They scorn my plastic
snake and sand-filled owl.

We cluck over their
white slimed droppings,
discarded oyster shells,
pink she-crab claws.

Our dock is the world to:
a duck in her wire straw nest;
swallows swirling underneath;
my leaky thrice-patched canoe;
kids who clamber the ladder
glued with gaping barnacles.

I lie drowsy, sun torn,
on vibrating planks,
watching ospreys fish,
purple martins snare
mosquitoes, mallards flirt,

and reflect on life
without wings, with glue,
(job, taxes, aging parents)
but also soaring flights.

Pumpkin Flowers

Yellow blossoms glow
between large fans of
leaves. Vines spill
past nasturtium bounds
into the shaggy lawn.

I should mow, weed,
neaten my unkempt Eden.
But pumpkin tendrils
grab the passive grass,
strangling out sun.

Morning glories ride
my fences, violet
blossoms radiating dawn,
spreading sunrise up
into the tree above.

Their heart-shaped leaves
tangle the baby tomatoes;
I snip their life lines.

How do you choose between
the flower and the fruit?

A young tulip poplar
shoots up strait
shading golden mums.
Too close to my home,
his roots threaten bricks.
Finally, I chainsaw him down.

In therapy I also dig,
scoop at resistance or
rake memories towards the dawn.

I edge the boundaries on
the psychiatric ward,
locking doors,
granting passes,
keeping blades away
from soft untended arms.

In an herb garden,
stray tomatoes become
weeds to be pulled,
so dill can wave green
feathers at the sky.

May my hands fertilize
medicinal leaves,
sweet berries and
glory-giving blooms.

Notes on the Death of a Deer

Swans roost on laps of waves,
yell at sun and terns.
We spill onto February's beach,
Two gifts: a thaw,
and my new love is here.
Snowdrops bob through brown leaves.
Green wheat sweeps the fields.
Ospreys dive in shafts of wind.

But, a duck blind sprouts horns
between unbeaten poles and juniper.
A flock of painted duck
decoys ride the waves.

Local men hunt, grow tobacco,
scrape oysters from hard beds.
In the city, we have rank;
here, only orange vests
shield us from country fire.

I shout. My love stumbles.
Do hunters aim
at our muscled hearts?
Buzzards flap and rise.
He steps onto the carcass
of a stag tethered by sand.

A fresh kill, swarmed by sandflies.
One antler with eight points
aloft; the other horn
under ground oyster shells.

Was he killed here,
or, bleeding, parched,
straggle to the river to die?

His eye, fixed, shrouds his killing.
No boats behind the blind.
Red-winged blackbirds claim reeds.
Swans, heedless, bob on.
Murder guts my throat.
My fingers twitch, wish
for a trigger to return rage.

That buck led his does
through holly and cedar
to raid butter winter lettuce.
I watched him from my window
as, sleepless, I wrestled
with my husband's betrayal.
My son called him "Rudolph."

I'd hoped this farm was sacred,
shielded by posted signs.
How do other mothers feel
when their children are shot?

I do not cry when we leave;
it's only a goddamn deer.

My black cat was run over
when I was twelve.
She slept on my head,
protected me. I'm grown,
there is no safety left.

Korean POW

1950—
Ten days into my tour,
our battalion aid station was
overrun by soldiers with a
red star, while I was staying
back with the wounded.
They were executed
with shots to the head.

I was thus captured, and
marched for weeks through
frozen turf, uniforms in shreds,
shoes stolen, in the Korean winter.

Hell could not be more vicious.
Those who fell out were
killed. Finally, we arrived
at prison camps in the far
north, where scant life
remained, except our captors.

The Chinese lectured about the evils of capitalism as we
huddled on wooden benches.
Frozen bones and skin,
our buddies, were piled
like cordwood, outside the huts.

For Thanksgiving, we boiled
five cabbages among fifty men.
When I awoke, so cold,
corpses surrounded me.

I used pliers to remove
teeth, but could not help
dysentery, dementia, dying.

1953—
We were liberated and
shipped back home.
My wife, and her toddler,
stared at my ribs and skull.

The newspapers called us
collaborators, because
we had survived.

What should I have done,
given up and died?
Sometimes, I wish I had.
But I have a family now.

Korean Birds
Yongsan Army Base, Seoul

In the land of the morning calm,
the evening din is raucous.

Blue-and-black magpies squawk,
quarrel for sticks to
festoon bulbous nests;
trains burrow underground,
helicopters churn overhead.

An asylum of my parents' America
survives on this military base:
school girls swing hands,
men tend grills of flamed burgers,
wives shop for peanut butter.

Long barrels hover
thirty miles north,
steel egg shells of
nerve-blocking gas,
threatening to hatch carnage
and drop a sea of fire.

When my father served here,
pulled from college in 1962
to decrypt communist codes,
trees were stumped by shells,
rubble and white crosses.
No bird song.

Plants and birds now
rise hopefully, but
old Koreans still walk
bent and bowed,
frail from a childhood of
tank-scarred rice fields.

Proud grandchildren riot,
pour kerosene on
stronger bodies
(flaming, falling)
to reunite their divorced mountain land.

At the army hospital
we play war games,
plan for mass casualties,
give orders in gas masks,
file with flashlights
into the bunker built by
Japanese conquerors.

Ring-necked pheasants,
red, green and gold,
strut about our barracks
like arrogant generals.
They call cadence on my roof,
eat bread crumbs I scatter,
scuttle at choppers.

We have one pilot dead,
one captured up north.
What birds does
the living man hear?

Magpies battling to tear
at his dead friend's eyes,
or golden pheasants
crying to mate again?

Fireballs Inside the Pentagon

A sphere of jet fuel flame clung
to the wall above my desk as
my office mate was draped with fire.
Smoke raced through the halls and
I could not see where or if to run.

Voices called and shrieked, and
I followed, to cooler halls.
"Go, Go, follow me!"
I made it to the courtyard.

But Lisa didn't. Nor John.
Nor one-hundred eighty two
other humans (and five highjackers).
I should have run back.
Lisa had a two-year old.
John—three kids.

They tell me I am a hero, simply
because I was in that wedge.
I don't feel that way—charred and
blistered, maybe, but only a little,
not enough to forgetwhat
I could have, should have done.

We dropped bombs on mountain caves.
They don't bring back my friends.
The Middle East has erupted.

Academic Conference in a Combat Zone
Baghdad, February 2004

Formerly "the Mecca of Arab medicine," now, after thirty years of wars and sanctions, the health system in Iraq needs enormous support. Planned by the US military and Iraqi physicians, and funded by the Agency for International Development (AID), the Iraqi Medical Specialist Forum was the first international medical conference in Iraq since the fall of Saddam Hussein. This event constituted an initial attempt for physicians from the United States to help their Iraqi counterparts upgrade their own specialty societies.

Our delegation of thirty doctors included practitioners from all over the United States in a range of disciplines. We were mainly strangers to each other. Some were Iraqi-American physicians returning "home" for the first time in decades. I am a military psychiatrist, but my role here was to represent the American Psychiatric Association.

Before I headed to Iraq for the three-day conference, designed to re-connect Iraqi physicians to the rest of the academic world, I had two primary concerns. What do I bring? How do I carry it? Via e-mail conversations, I was told that rolling suitcases don't work well there.

So I packed everything—business suits, head scarves, my desert camouflage uniform and boots, thirty CDs, clothes for going to museums in Amsterdam and camel-riding in Jordan during the layovers—into soft-sided bags I could schlep. Flak jackets and Kevlar helmets would be loaned to us at the airport in Baghdad.

After a pleasant day layover in Amsterdam, and a few hours in Amman, we flew on a military C-130 plane from Jordan to Baghdad, over barren brown desert with an occasional empty road in the sand. During the spiraling descent of the C-130, we were tense. The flak vest and helmets were heavy, but we all wore them for the bus trip from the airport to the Green Zone, along the infamous airport road, known for mines and snipers.

The Green Zone refers to the area of Saddam's palaces, the Ba'athist party headquarters, and other gorgeous villas belonging to the former party in power. Now the Coalition Provisional Authority (CPA) and other headquarters units are housed in Saddam's palace. We lugged our gear over cracked pavement and past concertina wire to the pool in the back of the palace.

Local Iraqis seldom visited the Green Zone, as it was tightly controlled. There are beautiful villas and pools, with charming bridges and swimming ducks. The troops now eat in the dining room of the palace, where, I was told, Sadaam used to poison selected of his guests. The "chapel" has large murals of rockets being fired towards the United States and Israel.

The other female physician on the delegation and I were billeted in the pool house. Like the palace, it was lined with marble, and the toilets and bidets have gold-plated handles. Ornate mirrors hang on the walls. Late in the evenings, I read under the palm trees by the pool, to the sound of intermittent gunfire.

Seven hundred Iraqi physicians from twenty medical societies registered for the conference. However, it was moved at the last minute from "Medical City" to a Conference Center in the Green Zone, because of intelligence about threats to our meeting. The Iraqi physicians had to pass through numerous checkpoints to enter, which often made them late. By attending, they risked being tarred as "collaborators."

Panels were held on specialty societies, malpractice, medical ethics, women's health issues, and numerous other subjects. I gave talks on forensic psychiatry and mental health and mass violence. It was clear that standards for informed consent were very different between our two cultures. During the malpractice talk, conversation revolved about the ethics of repairing a hymen before a woman was to be married.

The conference center was next to the Al-Rasheed Hotel, notorious because rockets hit it while Paul Wolfowitz was staying there. One of our military hosts had been severely injured in that attack. The hotel no longer houses guests on the upper floors, but the restaurant is still open. The food was good. I bought forty dinar bills with Sadaam's picture for five dollars at the bazaar. Prominent signs led to an Attack Shelter in the basement.

We quickly desensitized to the sound of gunfire. Some shots, we were told, were fired into the air for celebrations, but many were clearly fired at the nearby gates leading into the Green Zone. Shells occasionally landed inside the gates. The trailers where the male doctors were staying were referred to as "buttertops."

In the first two days, some of my colleagues visited local hospitals, without incident. On the third day, two Iraqi doctors invited two pediatricians (Larry and Ed) from Mass General and myself to visit "Medical City." After discussion with local military staff, we accepted—a chance to see "the real" Baghdad.

So the pediatricians, the two Iraqi doctors and I took military sponsored buses out of the Green Zone to the Babylon Hotel. From there, our friends took us by their car to "Medical City." The insane traffic seemed the main threat. Few paid any attention our presence inside the car.

Along the way we passed the bombed towers and the looted museum. The rest of the city was brown and decrepit, but showed little overt damage from the recent war.

The ER of the pediatric hospital demonstrated all that our Iraqi counterparts had been telling us—dirty facilities, no nurses, and very sick children. The parents did not seem to mind our presence, and appeared grateful that we hovered over the beds and palpated the bloated stomach of a child with hydronephrotic syndrome.

We next saw a typical medical office—full of dust, one book, and no computer. It did have a window. The bathroom, which by now I desperately needed, was the typical "squat and pee." At least I did not have to touch anything.

The Emergency Room of Baghdad Teaching Hospital was also sparse. The staff welcomed us, and we saw a few patients, including a "Tegretol poisoning." I did not get to learn more about her, because two children were carried in, injured by a bomb. One girl was severely wounded and covered with blood. The other was already dead.

We left to continue our tour of Medical City's hospitals outside. One of our hosts pointed out where, in the early days of the US occupation, he had negotiated with the Marines to keep the hospital safe. He also showed us the sparse plot of grass where unidentified bodies from the conflict were buried.

Coming up past the low wall between the Tigris and the hospital, I heard what I thought were rockets. My host reassured me that it was only a "celebration." I followed him up past the entrance to Baghdad Teaching Hospital.

Suddenly, Larry slapped my back hard. "Cameron, Cameron, hurry up. I just saw a red spot on your back! Move!"

We trotted back to the car. Larry reiterated that a red laser beam —from a sniper's scope—was focused first on Ed's shoes and then on my back.

We jumped into our hosts' car and headed back towards the Green Zone, driving through a busy street, which showcased the emergence of capitalism. A truck full of men with guns idled next to us—but they were guests from a wedding party. I felt jammed into the mass of cars, and wanted to get back to the relative safety of the Zone.

Our friends dropped us off at the gate. I had previously negotiated that we would not linger to say goodbye there, as gates were dangerous places. Nevertheless, they wanted to shake our hands to say goodbye. I ducked off behind the concrete barrier to retrieve my pass and passport.

After getting cleared and walking past the concrete barriers, we realized that our hosts had left us at the wrong gate, not the one near the Al-Rasheed Hotel. I asked the helmeted soldier how long it would take us to walk there. "Wait for a safe ride," he urged.

So we hunkered down behind the armored personnel carrier on the bridge. We all knew that it was at the checkpoints where shots were fired and bombs set off. Eventually a contractor gave us a ride to the hotel.

At dinner in the restaurant, we learned that a cluster bomb had been found under the podium of the conference hall in Baghdad Teaching Hospital, where we had just spent the afternoon. Two US soldiers were killed that day, one in Baghdad and the other further south. A car containing four American Baptist ministers was also ambushed, and one died.

The next day, Larry chastised me for having seemingly trivialized the "red dot" on my back. Since I did not see it, I was not overly perturbed. After all, I pointed out, our soldiers get targeted all the time.

The security officer on the bus told the group that three physicians had been watched the whole time and targeted by a sniper. I did not correct him. Further visits to Medical City were "strongly discouraged."

The story spread like wildfire at the conference. I politely refused other invitations to go out for dinner or tours. Other American physicians were disappointed that their professional contacts were curtailed, but they understood. Nobody wanted the forum to be ruined by news of one of our deaths.

The rest of the conference went without a hitch. The Iraqi physicians appeared very energized by our visit there. Many want to come train in the United States. The lectures were well received, but the networking was the most important. I ran out of business cards. I wanted to stay a few more days, but it was time to go. Our pockets were stuffed with slips of paper with e-mail addresses and our suitcases with baklava.

The question was how to leverage our visit into a lifeline to help them reclaim their rich medical heritage? And how to develop specialty society bylaws, train nurses, obtain quality pharmaceuticals, get needed medical equipment, and provide much needed further training to the physicians?

On the return ride to the airport, back in flak vests, we were much calmer than on our arrival. During the take-off, however, the C-130 rolled wildly to deflect rockets, which left me a little white-knuckled. We took photos of ourselves in the back of the plane, in front of the American flag, with a handsome member of the flight crew from the Hollywood National Guard.

When we arrived in Jordan, I was glad to be out of Iraq. But I want to go back: so much unfinished business.

We were also sorry to split up from each other. Our delegation had arrived as strangers and left as battle buddies. Safely home, I missed them. Fortunately, there were e-mails and photos from Iraqi physicians and my fellow travelers on my computer screen.

Black Uniform Ties

I went to the uniform store
at Ft. Myers to update my
dress blues with new rank and
maroon ribbon on the sleeve.

The war in Iraq and the abuse
pictures define my days, though I
have only briefly been to Baghdad.

A sergeant approached the saleswoman
and asked, "How many ties
do you have in stock?"
"How many," she asked, "do you need?"
"All that you have."

I looked quizzical.
He showed me his ID card.
Mortuary affairs.

"They've run out at Dover.
The Marines are coming in."

At the checkout counter, he bore
thirty ties, and as many Class A jackets
as he could carry.

I drove out slowly, beside
Humvees and Arlington Cemetery,
where my grandfather lies,
while the sound of taps
streamed by the glowing daffodils.

Ghosts of Abu Ghraib

Pictures electrified the world.
Orange suited prisoners in
black hoods with electrodes to
their testicles. What evil.

I visited Abu Ghraib, a desert hell.
On the eight-mile convoy from Baghdad
I pointed my pistol out the window
of the unarmored HUMVEE,
not knowing whether my body would
still have two legs and the end of the trip.

The past is gruesome.
30,000 deaths, gallows or
pistol shots, for the lucky.
If Saddam's executioners liked you
"they fed you head first
to the chopper, otherwise,
you went in feet first."

Meat hooks adorn our ceiling
where the four of us sleep,
trying to ignore the loud snoring
and the mortar attacks.

Through the wire, we talk to detainees,
A few suicidal, or at least
determined to cut their necks and arms,
too easy given the concertina wire,
with triangular razor edges.

"I am innocent," all the detainees say.
"And my mother is very sick."
They open their mouth to show
decayed teeth, hoping for dentists.

The medical staff do the best they can.
Five hours of sick call through the wire
with the hot sun beating on them
in flak jackets and Kevlar helmets.

All conscious of the scandal,
trying to do the best they can
despite sunburn and sweat
dripping through every pore.

The mortars land.
Last April they killed 22 detainees,
They keep coming.

At night the choppers sweep in by twos.
kicking up dust and human bones,
dropping off insurgents while
lines of soldiers wait on their backpacks
in the landfill. And the bats fly.

I see Saddam's death chamber:
the double gallows where flames
were lit under the condemned,
who had scrawled their names
and dates of execution on the wall.

The evil is thick.
We erred, we sinned.
But the ghosts of Abu
demand a reckoning.

Heart of Darkness: A Visit to Abu Ghraib

We went to the prison to do an assessment of mental health needs of soldiers and detainees. This essay cannot report on those findings, as that is yet to be released. This is a description of the experience visiting the prison to of gather information. It was mainly written by the light of the computer outside, while swapping at mosquitoes. My computer now is coated with dust. (Later, back in the States, it crashed.)

Recently selected for the job of Psychiatry Consultant to the Army Surgeon General, I went to the prisons to assess the mental health needs of soldiers and detainees.

We gathered for the convoy on the outskirts of BIAP, the Baghdad International Airport. There was a gathering line of Humvees, armored SUVs, and gunships. The soldiers were smoking and joking, leaning on their vehicles.

We were on the way to Abu Ghraib. Eight long miles through one of the most dangerous routes in Iraq. The main supply route we were to travel was "green," but we still got the warning about explosive devices, roadside bombs, and instructions to point our weapons out the windows of the vehicle. I had my photo taken with the young female captain who would be driving, and joked to Todd that this might be the last photo with both my legs. (Our Humvees was not armored.) Fortunately, it was not the last photo.

My silly 9 mm pistol pointed out the window for the long twenty minutes it takes us to get there, we reached the infamous prison, a large walled compound in the suburbs of Baghdad.

They showed us to our sleeping quarters, a large empty room with some file cabinets, with records of detainee health care.

We set up our cots. It had been ten years since Somalia that I put together a cot, and had to ask our NCO to help. (That NCO also snored very loudly.)

Soldiers are lodged in the prison cells, literally. "Kids" in gray Army t-shirts have turned cells into home with plywood doors and mink blankets. They walk to the chow hall in their desert camouflage uniform (DCUs) or Army gym clothes, plus body armor and helmet.

Always one has to wear flak jackets and Kevlar helmets when outside the hardened facilities. Weapons and magazines with bullets must always be within easy reach. Two rockets landed not far away today, and another few the day before.

Last April multiple mortars landed in the tents of the detainees. In one attack, 22 Iraqis were killed and a hundred more wounded. The MPs could not get help for a long while, because the detainees were throwing stones at them. The rockets had US on their fins.

The whole place is a trash dump, literally built on a landfill. Perhaps 19,000 people were killed there in the last decade, or only 12,000, or maybe 30,000, or 100,000 depending upon with whom you talk. Occasionally the boots of the soldiers' kick up human bones.

Hooks are screwed in to on the ceiling in the cells, and in the large common room where we have put up cots. Prisoners were strung up there during Saddam's reign. Now the hooks serve to string ponchos, separating girl and boy soldiers.

"The place is full of evil spirits," said the rational doctor across from me on at the plywood diner table at chow. They say that if you take photos in the death chamber, shadowy faces of the dead will appear in the edges of the picture.

A young medic gave me a tour of our living quarters, one of the prison buildings. Standing on the roof, my guide points out where they think insurgents will attempt to breach the walls. Trash used to be piled up to the roof, a perfect landing platform. The medics, who live within the prison for security from the rockets, have made plans to secure the LSA (living space area) in the event that insurgents attack inside their living quarters.

I was not sure that I have confidence in the plan. But I just got here.

That first night, I sleep soundly. I vaguely hear some thuds, then a siren. They call us to put on our flak jackets and Kevlar helmets. We assemble in formation, then go back to bed. A couple more thuds—mortars or helmets hitting the floor?

Next morning at staff meeting we learn that five mortars landed within the compound walls. Some damage to the motor pool, no one hurt.

In the morning, I visited the compounds on sick call and did psychiatric rounds, "through the wire." The detainees live 200 to 300 in a compound. Through an interpreter we ask the identified "psych patients" about their symptoms of anxiety and depression.

With my body armor on, and the 120 degrees temperature, I drip sweat continually. So do the guards, with their heavier guns. I am beat after an hour. The air-conditioned wooden shacks of the guards and chilled water offer relief.

So many poignant stories from detainees:

"My mother died when I was here, I could not go home to bury her."

"I was with my father and brother and cousins, and they made me come in here (with the other juveniles). Please let me go back to my family. I am more comfortable there."

"I am a geologist, and my sister and uncles are doctors. The Americans treat us well here. I want to work for them when I am released."

"I want to go back to the hospital. I will swallow some more razor blades (from the concertina wire) if I cannot go back."

"When am I going to be released?" is the universal question from all the detainees.

Are their stories true? The guard reminds me that they come from the insurgents, who have tried to kill my fellow soldiers.

Thirty-six juveniles are imprisoned there, aged 12 to 18. They say they are older, in order to rejoin their families.

There are also stories from the correctional staff, hard-working soldiers, also in flak and Kevlar, plus many weapons. It is hot, but they seem to have adjusted to the desert. It is other issues that they talk about.

"My son was killed right before I came out here. I wanted to come here; otherwise I would have killed the guy who did it. Now I need to go back for his trial."

" I don't want to report it…in the convey, he kept taking my hand and putting it in my crotch…. my mother was a marine for 20 years, she tells me to just hang."

"They point their fingers imitating RPGs at me, shout Fallujah, and threaten my family."

But the guards seem to be doing all right, their main complaints are of the recent prison scandal, and how they are tarred by that brush.

In the evening, bats flit everywhere in the setting sun, which outlines the watchtower. This is the end of the first full day.

The choppers came and went all night. There were no more mortar attacks. But roadside bombs killed two American soldiers nearby.

The next morning, we went to the "hard site." The infamous photos of the naked human pyramids were taken here. Now the Iraqis are in charge, and the cells are used for "criminals." The cellblock is used for isolation. The cells are very small, and dark. Hands reach out through the bars, as in a hundred bad movies, but here it is for real. The contractors who lead us through seem sincere and motivated, and urge the Iraqi medical staff to attend to their prisoners. I see the morgue, currently empty.

Most prisoners seem grateful for the American presence. American contractors insist that the prisoners get treatment. But when the jail door opens, and there is only one Iraqi warden between the detainees with baleful stares and us, separated only by a warden and an open door, I decide to move on.

I do have a souvenir—an orange jump suit with Arabic writing on the back. Will I wear it on Halloween?

Saddam's death chamber has twin gallows. We view cells where prisoners waited to die, names and dates of execution scrawled on the wall in Arabic. The dates are clear.

How many died here? They say that if the guards liked you they fed you to the grinder headfirst, rather than feet first. It is hard for me to comprehend that much cruelty.

Our interpreter was imprisoned there for 3 years. He looked somewhat shell-shocked by being back in the "hard site."

Good care is now delivered to the wounded, the ill, those with gunshot wounds suffered in fights with our troops. Mental health care has just arrived. I have a tour of the new hospital—big, effective and clean.

More sick call in the camps. Detainees are colorfully dressed, praying together on large mats. We watch them pray and play volleyball from the watchtower where the soldiers break up fights with lethal or non-lethal weapons (rubber bullets).

The psych folks try to get people to take their meds, to not threaten to scratch themselves on concertina wire, or eat the sharp blades. Too many have swallowed them.

Coming back at night from the Internet café in my army shorts and shirt uniform, there is a dog barking balefully. Three soldiers have already been bitten and were given rabies shots. I only have sneakers and bare calves, can I kick him? Or shoot? I wish I had my boots on. My little clip-on penlight does not offer much light.

I watch as two Chinooks speed in, low and fast and with no lights. They land in the dark on the pad, swirling up sand into the lights from the prison. Soldiers have been sitting on the pad to bring the "insurgents' into the prison, to be interrogated.

Sounds: generators, dogs, cars, air conditioners, choppers, cars, no mortars.

Sights: prison lit up, choppers flying in low and dark, soldiers in the dark on the side of the road, waiting to board, a line of blindfolded men, ready for interrogation, the empty watchtower.

Feel: hot wind-blowing sand; sweat dripping down my neck, fingers typing on the computer keyboard.

Smells: porta-potties. No smell of death, not bad, unless imagined. But the whole place is a killing ground.

Uncertainty: whether there will be scorpions in the latrine, insurgents on the walls, rockets on our sleeping platforms, or if the snores from the NCO will keep me awake. This is an uncertain place.

Two days and three nights after arrival we get up at 5 AM to catch the convoy home. This time the security brief is more serious. Seven Marines were killed two days ago slightly west of here, and an IED exploded on this road last night. Weapons should be locked and loaded. "Watch out for friendlies though."

We do move out, speeding down the highway, guns again pointed out the window, past old cars and trucks and a new big pothole from an IED that was not there two days ago. Sheep and villages lie along the side. Then to a more rural road, with tall grass that could easily hide a sniper, and the pace is way too slow. A beautiful morning though, especially to be whole and alive.

Into the checkpoint, we clear our barrels, and we are safe inside the compound.

Back at home, I show pictures to an Iraqi-American colleague, whose thirteen cousins were executed by Saddam, three of whom were at Abu.

My computer will not turn on, and I blame ghosts or sand from Abu Ghraib. A very evil place.

The Terrorist Tick

She worried about me when
I was sent to Abu Ghraib. I returned
unscathed. But there are djinns.

My mother, a lithe redhead who
earned an orange belt in karate,
published ten books,
slammed tennis balls for two hours a day,
taught poetry to the children of oystermen,
now cannot raise her head from the hospital bed.

It's the "Osama Tick," she joked
before the flaccid paralysis robbed her
of humor. Then she repeatedly apologized
for weakness, prejudice, and leaking stool.

The granddaughter of a Russian general,
she bossed me around. We fought over
"who's in charge," at the helm of
our new sailing dinghy. Finally,
my daughter and I jumped overboard,
braving the tentacles of jellyfish,
leaving her to savor breezes and ospreys.

Now she wants me to go
so that she can sleep.
My kids are do not understand.

The titers are high for Erlichiosis,
A disease borne by ticks.
Although a physician,
I am ignorant of that zebra.

I learn quickly. Demand, indeed, fight
with her doctors. Insist on a spinal tap.
Transfer her to Hopkins,
where they diagnosed ADEM,
Acute disseminated encephalomyelitis.

The MRI shows white tentacles
throughout her brain. Ghosts
from a toxic tick,
though it is not yet Halloween.

She knows the president when asked:
"that horrible man." But keeps restating
"I am a mound of flesh."
Thinks she is a guinea pig.
Christ, the neediness in her voice!

Steroids fight back. She improves.
Transfers to rehab. Can walk with help.
The crisis is over. She is alive
but bemoans the loss of her ability
to run to the dock, write, or feed
her husband and needy white cat.

So I will write poems for her, and judge
the waves until she can be the captain.
She needs to be in charge again, and
scuttle that tick.

The Swan Feathers Castle

Jessie and I kayak through the slapping
fall waves in our red kayak,
slip paddles into the gold-leaved cove.
Two royal swans glare at our approach.

We pull into the shallow beach,
tracked with shallow trails of
festive otters, bold deer, shore birds.
Swan feathers are tangled in
the stems of desiccated weeds.

Our purple bucket and yellow shovel
are the power tools to create the
sand base of our pop-up mansion.

We find magic white feathers to make
the halo of sails atop the sloping roof,
a challenge to the Sydney Opera House.

A shell path, between wildflower stems
becomes the entrance to the world of
the seaweed people, dancing in their
magic ballroom, to the sounds of frivolous
crabs playing violins on their claws.

The swans approach, pennants unfurled,
demanding either their feathers or our flesh.
We retreat, herons beating their blue-grey
anthems to the beat of the military waves.

Army Surgeon, 2006

I have operated non-stop
for five months now
on infantrymen, insurgents,
children missing
arms, legs and eyes.

When the shift ends, I lie
on my cot. Gross wounds
re-appear under my eyes.
Incoming mortars also
erupt my scattered dreams.

My second tour in the sandbox.
Soon I go home. I do not know
where my peace lies.
Here I try to repair bombed
bodies, broken minds.

Back there, I fill out forms,
prepare for JACHO, and
try to talk to my wife and kids.
Shopping does not interest me.
Nor do malls, or hair styles.

One of my medics
was killed last week.
I only could recognize him by
the name on his toe tag.
He threw himself across his patient.
Both dead now.

War advances surgery.

A general surgeon,
I have done incredible
operations on injuries
I never saw before.

I snuck out the back door
of the tent and sobbed
when I could not save a
two-year-old girl
with long lustrous eyelashes.

Should I volunteer to stay
another rotation?
I am needed here.
I am an Army Surgeon.
This is my calling.

Detainee, Guantanamo Bay, Cuba

It is not a jail, but a religious school,
or so I wrote to family.
Better than Bagram, or the hut
where I grew up, herding goats.

Here I learn the religious tenets
out in the recreation yard
And I am a master at stopping up
my toilet and flooding my cell.

We taunt our guards, fling feces,
complain of torture to the ICRC
and defense attorneys.
The Inn in Cuba, we call it privately.

The doctors so seriously inquire
about depression and that PSTD—whatever.
They ignore my "burning heart,"
that stomach pain I get when I eat.
So I don't.

I do miss my parents, and send them
greetings at Eid. I love the M&Ms
the interrogators provide—what fools
they are! Thinking I will sell UBL
for a chocolate bar and a cup of Starbucks.
I will go an a hunger strike today.

For a new life in England, on the other hand,
I would cheerfully betray all I know.
I will not get that life.
I don't want to return to herding goats.
So I refuse the trial. "Illegal, oppression!"

The ocean is blue and wide,
iguanas and banana rats
are outside the wire netting.

I wish I were free, in England.

Army Medicine

I have been an Army doctor for 24 years.
Treated and written about Soldiers,
fighting, scared, wounded and dead.

I have spent time in the mud in Korea,
eaten sand and hung with camels in Mogadishu,
witnessed the 9/11 attacks on the Pentagon.

The litany goes on:
they targeted me in the streets of Baghdad,
later I hung low in a chopper crossing
the sands of Iraq while a harvest moon
hung red and round over the desert.

I write about Soldiers, but I am one too.
Shot at infrequently, more often simply
sick of sandstorms or missing
home and kids or a cold Diet Coke.

Images cross my eyeballs:
the fireballs outside the Pentagon,
taps at Arlington Cemetery,
another burned Iraqi child,

And notes, and smells.
More taps, sweet dung from horses
drawing the caissons of our dead.

Biography
COL Elspeth Cameron Ritchie, MD, MPH

COL Ritchie just concluded five years as the Director of the Proponency of Behavioral Health Director at the Office of the US Army Surgeon General. She has held numerous leadership positions within Army Medicine, to include the Psychiatry Consultant. She trained at Harvard, George Washington, Walter Reed, and the Uniformed Services University of the Health Sciences, and has completed fellowships in both forensic and preventive and disaster psychiatry. She is a Professor of Psychiatry at the Uniformed Services University of the Health Sciences.

An internationally recognized expert, she brings a unique public health approach to the management of disaster and combat mental health issues. Her assignments and other missions have taken her to Korea, Somalia, Iraq, and Cuba. She has over 130 publications, mainly in the areas of forensic, disaster, suicide, ethics, military combat and operational psychiatry, and women's health issues.

Major publications include "The Mental Health Response to the 9/11 Attack on the Pentagon", "Mental Health Interventions for Mass Violence and Disaster" and "Humanitarian Assistance and Health Diplomacy: Military-Civilian Partnership in the 2004 Tsunami Aftermath". She is currently the senior editor on the forthcoming Combat and Operational Behavioral Health, the Textbook of Forensic Military Mental Health, and the Therapeutic Use of Canines in Army Medicine.

Other Books from The Wineberry Press

Listening for Wings, by Maxine Combs

Horse and Cart: Stories from the Country, by Elisabeth Stevens

Get With it, Lord, by Beatrice M. Murphy

No One is Listening, by Elizabeth Follin-Jones

20/20 Visionary Eclipse & the Whorling Try/Angles,
                                 by Judith McCombs

Finding the Name, an anthology, editor Elisavietta Ritchie

THE WINEBERRY PRESS